How to Share CHRIST Confidently

A Guide to Comfortable and Effective Personal Witnessing

Introduction

Christians receive a lot of encouragement to share their faith and to be effective personal witnesses—serious Christians take this seriously. My impression is that most Christians really want to be good witnesses. They want to introduce others to Jesus or draw them closer to Him. They may even have tried. However, in too many instances, trying to witness turns out to be a frustrating and uncomfortable experience. For others, the prospect of witnessing is so unsettling that they cannot bring themselves even to try. Consequently, a tragically large percentage of Christian believers rarely, if ever, say anything to anyone about Jesus in a personal way, and rarely, if ever, give personal testimony about their Lord and Savior.

There are reasons for this hesitancy, of course. Some are personal, such as shyness, lack of knowledge and communication skills, weak motivation, or pessimism. Above all, there is fear. But there is also a significant spiritual dimension to our reluctance to share Jesus. Satan's strategy is to exaggerate the difficulties in witnessing and to minimize our God-given potential and opportunities.

Satan also distorts our perception of the truth. He lies to us and assures us that it really is not necessary to say anything to others about the One who gave His all for them, about the One who urgently longs to rescue them and be close to them. Satan would like us to believe that, in the end, all will be saved—whether they believe in Jesus or not. After all, a loving and merciful God would have it no other way. Of course, the Bible says the opposite, clearly and emphatically: "Whoever believes in Him [Jesus] is not condemned, but whoever does not believe is condemned already, because he has not believed in the name of the only Son of God" (John 3:18).

These factors, the personal as well the spiritual, are what inhibit us from sharing Christ as comfortably and effectively as we could. They form a tough, seemingly impenetrable barrier of inhibition. Or, to modify the image, they are like a net in which a victim is trapped. The victim struggles. The net gives but will not tear, preventing the captive from escaping into the freedom once enjoyed.

But by the work of Christ we have been set free—free from the corrupting and condemning consequences of sin, free from Satan's control, free to love and trust and serve God. That also means free to share Christ confidently, joyfully, and readily, as we were meant to do.

Still, the net of inhibition remains—eager to entrap us, to deprive us of the high privilege and joy of liberating others by introducing them to Jesus. But God has provided us with effective instruments of escape. We can cut through that net of inhibition and become more comfortable and effective in sharing Christ.

God enables us to understand what inhibits our witness, and even more important, He also enables us to improve. This book offers help in using the resources God has provided. What follows is not a quick fix. It is a guide through which, under God's blessing, we can keep growing in that vital ministry of sharing the Good News. We will examine the major components of the witness experience, analyze what can prevent or impair effective testimony, and then explore the resources that enable and empower it.

The following pages offer the aspiring Christian witness information, encouragement, skills, and support, as well as a method for successful problem solving. The beliefs and values incorporated here are based on scriptural truth. The practical applications are based on many years of personal witnessing, as well as extensive study, teaching, and writing about this vital aspect of the Christian life. However, I cannot present myself as an accomplished or model Christian witness. I have a need and desire to keep learning. Although I share some witness experiences that seemed to go well, there were many that did not.

Saying an effective word about Jesus can be spontaneous and natural. However, it is usually done intentionally and can be learned. It is best learned not just from a book or in a classroom but in real-life experience. For this reason, at the end of each chapter there will be a section on putting these lessons into practice. Actually doing these exercises is important, even essential, to the growth experience. Another suggestion is to keep a personal journal. Recording your experiences in a journal allows you to capture the moment and becomes a means of encouragement as you record challenges and solutions, problems and progress.

1
Desensitization

Dealing with Our Fear of Witnessing

Probably the single greatest deterrent to personal and informal sharing of the Gospel is fear. Even strong, capable, well-informed, and experienced believers admit to fear that approaches panic when faced with a situation in which they realize that they could and should say something about their Savior. People with excellent verbal skills choke into silence when their witness is needed. I personally know several people who give large sums of money to support others in evangelism and mission ministry because they are afraid to bear witness themselves. That silent majority of believers, held captive with sealed lips, is caught in the net of fear.

A. The Fears That Silence

What, exactly, are we afraid of? High on the fear list is **rejection**, the big NO—not only no to Jesus but also no to us personally. We risk alienating others and becoming isolated. Certain people may not wish to associate with us if we witness to them. Relationships can suffer and break when witnessing is introduced. Our job or business or social life could suffer. Religion is a sensitive and personal matter, and people become uncomfortable when it is introduced. It can even be offensive, especially if we assert that there is only one way to God and salvation and that Jesus is that way. The world's political correctness requires that we regard all religions as equally valid. Confronted with the opportunity to tell someone about Jesus, the fear of failure and rejection often keep us speechless.

Inadequacy is another major issue. We just do not know what to say or how to say it. We do not say anything about Jesus because we are afraid that we will botch it or come out with something false or stupid, with the result that we will do more harm than good. We feel that we lack the information and confidence needed to witness. Despite all the preaching and teaching that we have absorbed, despite all the reading we have done in the Bible and other fine Christian literature, we are afraid that we just do not have anything to say, at least not the right thing. We dread the embarrassment of being tongue-tied or incoherent in a witness situation.

The fear of ridicule also generates anxiety. For some reason, being sneered or jeered at, especially about our faith, can be even more devastating than a physical blow. The mockery and insults that were hurled at Jesus from every direction during His crucifixion were almost as painful as the wounds inflicted by whip, thorns, and nails. The possibility of being put down by someone with whom we have tried to share our faith is intimidating. Who wants to be regarded as weird or ignorant or out of step with the culture? You try to tell someone about your deepest convictions, about the One who means more to you and does more for you than anyone else, and the response is a contemptuous, pitying look that says, "You are pathetically and hopelessly deluded." That would be hard to take, so hard that we would rather not take the chance.

B. Counteracting Fear

We are not going to make much progress in personal witnessing unless we deal with the fear factors. And we can address them effectively. We can break out of the net of inhibition and reluctance that so often surrounds us, preventing us from carrying out our vital, God-given assignment to speak up for Him. These fears are very real to us. They are strong and disabling, but they can be overcome.

Once they are overcome, we can experience the meaningful, rewarding, fulfilling, even exhilarating feeling of having pleased and honored God, of having warmed His heart and put a smile on His face. The reason why it affects Him that way is that when we tell others about Jesus, we are touching them with His love. Our Lord urgently wants people to know Him, love Him, and trust Him, so that He can help them with their deepest needs. For that to happen, they have to know Jesus and what He has done for them. That is our high privilege: to deliver the Good News to people, the news that they matter to God more than they realize, that He has help for them right now and hope for a fabulous future.

St. Paul makes a stirring case for the necessity and privilege of proclaiming Jesus, and it applies to personal witnessing as well as the preaching that he mentions: "How are they to believe in Him of whom they have never heard? And how are they to hear without someone preaching? . . . As it is written, 'How beautiful are the feet of those who preach the good news' " (Romans 10:14b, 15b).

Do Not Take Your Fears Too Seriously

If you have struggled seriously but unsuccessfully against your fears, you will be tempted to give up. "It is no use. I just cannot do this. I cannot open my heart and mouth about Jesus. I am too afraid. I am ashamed of being so weak and fearful, but I cannot help it. That is just the way I am. If the people I contact need to hear about Jesus, someone else will have to do it. I will have to do the Lord's work some other way."

A person cannot simply ignore such feelings; they have to be addressed. No matter how strong, these feelings can be addressed successfully. Our ultimate confidence about this rests not in human resources of any kind but in God and the help that He provides. St. Paul writes, "I can do all things through Him who strengthens me" (Philippians 4:13). And echoing Christ, Paul says, "My power is made perfect in weakness" (2 Corinthians 12:9).

These are sweeping and thrilling promises. They tell us that we never have to cave in to these intimidating fears planted and nurtured in us by Satan. With God's help, through His mighty and ever-present Spirit within, we can prevail. We really can. Every time we hear or read His Word, every time we kneel in faith at His table, God's power is recharged within us. So, instead of living under a cloud of fear and failure, instead of responding out of a sense of defeat and submission to our fears, we can act out of confidence in God and in the victory that He has won over our fears. We can count on Him to repeat that victory over the fears that are paralyzing our witness.

There are also some psychological steps that can clear the way for God's victorious power to do its work. That is, **we can desensitize ourselves to these fears**. We can act on our fears in such a way that, though they may still cause discomfort, they will no longer be able to control us or prevent us from saying something about Jesus.

One way to do this is to **examine our fears rationally**. Ask yourself these questions: What is the worst thing that someone could do to me in reaction to my witness? How serious and lasting would my discomfort be if the response to my message was contempt or hostility? My own experience indicates that less than 5 percent of those who respond to witness do so in an ugly or insulting way, though, of course, many more decline politely. Contrast that with the 100 percent positive, even enthusiastic, reaction of God to even the humblest testimony about His Son. Consider also the fact that 100 percent of those to whom we offer Jesus and His saving work are touched by His love and Spirit whether they accept it or not. Doesn't this take some of the fear out of witnessing and call attention to its value?

Another way to be desensitized to our fears about speaking of Jesus is to **turn them into adventure**. Fear can add excitement to life. Think of the dangerous or scary thrills for which people pay handsomely: extreme sports, auto racing, roller coasters, and so on. A dose of fear pours adrenaline into the system and evokes a sense of success and satisfaction for enduring it. Fear can add a new dimension to our experience. Those who relish thrills speak of the "high" that they produce.

It is not a stretch to say that believers who break through the fear restraints and actually introduce someone to Jesus usually find it to be an exciting and rewarding adventure, even if the person to whom they witnessed was not very positive. The fear with which they approached the opportunity made it challenging in an exciting way. And the fact that they actually did it despite their fear, that as God's representative and with the support of His Spirit they offered someone God's richest and most precious gift, was fulfilling beyond their highest expectation. There is no question about it: sharing Christ is an exciting adventure and one that the witness wants to repeat.

Fear of witnessing can turn into an exciting and fulfilling adventure. It has happened to me and I have seen it happen to others. I was helping out as a small group leader at a large gathering of youth who were learning how to witness. After several hours of informative and inspirational presentations, they were to go out in groups of two or three to do door-to-door witnessing on the basis of some standard evangelism questions.

Two young women in my group were trembling with fear at the prospect and asked me if I would go with them. I agreed, explaining that they would not have to say anything themselves until and unless they really wanted to. All I asked was that they support my witnessing with prayer. When we had just two more homes left to visit, one of the girls mustered up the courage to announce that she would do the talking at these doors. I was as surprised as I was pleased.

With more confidence and warmth than I expected, she shared her Savior at these doors and was well received. The results were electrifying on all three of us. She did it! It was a thrilling adventure. She broke through the net of fear and offered these people what they needed more than anything else in the world. She may have changed their lives forever. In the process, I am convinced that the Lord also changed her forever.

Inadequacy is nothing to fear. Jesus is very emphatic about that. He explains that even when witnessing in the face of life-threatening hostility we do not have to worry about what to say because He Himself will provide the words (Luke 21:12–15). Notice that He does not discourage thoughtful preparation for testimony, only that we should not let fear of inadequacy stop us.

What could be more reassuring? What could more effectively counteract fear or even dispel it altogether? Jesus' promise holds true, even in non-threatening situations. This sounds almost too good to be true, and the enemy will do everything in his power to make us doubt it. However, the promises of Christ are always far more powerful than the devil's doubts. If we can count on Him to keep His supreme promises of forgiveness and eternal life through His sacrifice, can we not also count on Him to keep this promise to support our witness? In effect, Christ dares us to take Him at His word and give Him the opportunity to come through. This, too, will be exciting. We will not be disappointed in the outcome.

Dispel fear with love. Out of concern for others, grounded in God's incomparable love for you and for them, tell them what they need to know, even though the net of fear is trying to restrain you. Let concern for their spiritual and eternal welfare push right through your fear. Let this love have its way with you. Let it make you worry more about them than you do about yourself or what a bad experience might do to your ego. Believe that God's love can do that. We have His word for it from the apostle John: "There is no fear in love. But perfect love casts out fear. . . . We love because He first loved us" (1 John 4:18, 19). Trust in His promise that the right words to say will come and that His Spirit will go with those words into the heart of the hearer.

A number of years ago, just down the street from our home, something happened that vividly portrayed love that could not be stopped by fear. A car burst into flames. Inside, there were several passengers, including one elderly disabled woman. Those who could escaped the flames, but this woman could not get out. The terrifying flames were raging so furiously that none of the bystanders dared try to rescue her. Suddenly, a young man rushed through the crowd and flames and pulled the woman to safety at the cost of serious burns to his arms, face, and torso. As he was recovering, a reporter asked him, "How could you do this? Weren't you afraid of being burned yourself, even fatally?" He replied, "Of course I was afraid, but I couldn't just stand there and watch her die." As the passage in 1 John says: love casts out fear. Our love for others, growing out of God's sacrificial love for us, can effectively dispel our fear of sharing Christ with those who need Him.

Practice

There are ways in which we can deal effectively with fears that keep us from sharing Christ. We can actually desensitize ourselves to them by identifying, analyzing, and evaluating our fears. Then we can cut through them with God's truth and the power of His Spirit. This will not make them completely disappear, but it will enable us get past them into the inspiring experience of being God's agent in making a profound and eternal difference in the lives of those who need it.

Conduct an experiment with fear. Discover or create at least two opportunities for witnessing. In these situations:

1. Study your fear reaction carefully. Which of the types discussed above was most prominent? Imagine the worst thing that could happen, if you were to witness.
2. Apply each of the countermeasures given above. Carefully observe how each affected your feelings.
3. Attempt a simple witness. Note your reaction and those of the others.
4. Record this in a personal witness journal and, if you are doing this study in a group, for presentation there.

2
Motivation

Growing Our Desire to Witness

"Where there is a will, there is a way." We know how true this saying is. It has been demonstrated convincingly over and over again. About a month after I began my first pastorate, I had an unforgettable experience teach me that if someone really wants to, no matter how limited or unprepared he might be, he can witness magnificently. *If he really wants to . . .*

Billy, age 7, was the most disturbed and disturbing child in our little Sunday School in New York City's Lower East Side. He did not attend often, but when he did, it was a disaster. He did not seem to care about the Lord or His Word. The only thing Billy seemed to be interested in was causing trouble. He annoyed the other children, disrupted the lesson, and drove the teacher out of her mind. When he was absent, we breathed a sigh of relief.

Late one summer afternoon, the doorbell rang. Imagine my surprise to find Billy, hand in hand with a little girl about his age. "Billy, what in the world are you doing here?" I asked. Billy lived a mile or so away, and to get to my door, he and his friend walked across some of the busiest streets in the world at rush hour. Billy's answer shocked me. "Pastor, this is Celia. She doesn't know anything about Jesus. I brought her here so that you could tell her about Him."

After they were seated inside, I said something that surprised me almost as much as what Billy said. "You know about Jesus, Billy. Suppose you tell her." What made me say that is still a mystery to me, because I am not at all sure that I really believed it.

Without any hesitation, Billy did just that—much more winsomely and effectively than anything I could have said. "Celia, Jesus was the best man who ever was. He was nice to everyone. If they were sad, He cheered them up. If they were sick, He made them better. He even made some dead people come back to life. But some bad people took Him and hurt Him. They killed Him by nailing Him to a cross. But you know, Celia, He didn't have to let them do that. He was God and could have stopped them. But you know why He let them do this, Celia? He did it for us so that we wouldn't have to be punished for our sins."

With a pained look on her face, Celia responded, "Aw, He shouldn't have done that!" Billy then explained excitedly, "He didn't stay dead, Celia. He came back to life again and went to see His friends. Were they ever glad to see Him! After a while He went back to heaven. We can't see Him now, but, you know, He's still here with us. When we are good it makes Him happy; but when we are bad it makes Him sad. Someday He's going to come back so that we can see Him, and then He's going to take us to be with Him forever."

This is not fiction. It really happened just as I wrote about it. We thought that Billy did not care about the Lord and His Word. We thought he did not listen or learn anything. But he learned a lot and cared a lot, even while he was causing all that trouble. Billy had serious disadvantages. He was from a broken home, had a nervous twitch, a crippled arm, and an eating disorder. But he was as earnest, eager, and effective a Christian witness as I have ever known. Why? Various factors were involved as we shall see, but they all came together in a believing, loving **desire** to do it. Where there is a will, there is a way.

In chapter 1, we analyzed the factors that prevent us from sharing Christ and considered ways to overcome them. But this is only the beginning of the solution. We still need to know how we can be energized and stimulated for action. We have learned how to overcome our fear—to just get in the car and buckle up, so to speak. Next, we turn our attention to starting the engine. Motivation is what sets us in motion, what makes us want tell others about Jesus. It gives us the kind of will to share Christ that finds a way to do it.

God Instills the Motivation to Share

Because our reluctance is so stubborn, it takes a mighty surge of power to get us moving. God has such power, and He uses it to activate our impulse to share the Gospel. Essentially it is the power of His saving love. He does not want to motivate us through guilt or even through duty. Rather, He wins our hearts with an outpouring of compassionate, extravagant, and undeserved mercy in the self-offering of His Son. That love conveys the living, personal presence of His Holy Spirit, who acts on our hearts and minds and wills, creating the desire to tell someone something about Jesus. He generates in us the kind of will that can find a way to introduce others to Jesus. When we know God's love in Christ for what it is and take it seriously, we realize that it is too good to keep to ourselves. Others need His love too—desperately—and we can offer it to them. This was the realization and response that moved Billy to do and say those beautiful things. Now we look in more detail at other types of motivation that God instills in the Christian witness.

God-centered motivation. The first and highest type of motivation for all of the Christian life is that which focuses on God. This is especially the case with witnessing. The better we get to know what God is like and what He has done, the more ready and eager we become to respond to Him in what we think, say, and do. Despite its ruin by sin, this marvelous planet and all that is in it impresses us with His wisdom, creative power, and ongoing involvement. His marvelous gift of life and health to everyone, as well as His generosity in providing for and protecting us, stir our hearts. The compassion that led Him to get personally, even physically, involved in rescuing us from our sins through the sacrificial life and death and resurrection of Jesus evokes our profound gratitude. His eagerness to draw us to Himself in a close, personal relationship and to live permanently within us through His Spirit prompts love for Him.

This awareness of God moves us. It makes us want to call Him to the attention of others. The more we learn about Him through His Word, the more we experience His presence and love, the more ready and willing we are to tell others about Jesus. This is Good News, the best ever, and it is meant for everyone, because everyone needs desperately to hear it. It is our assignment and high privilege to deliver this Good News wherever possible. God is pleased and honored when we do this, and this makes it compelling to us. It is a joy to please and honor someone whom you love and to whom you are indebted, especially if that person is important. No praise means more to God than when we tell someone else how wonderful He is and how much His Son means to us. The apostle Peter puts this in thrilling words: "You are a chosen race, a royal priesthood, a holy nation, a people for His own possession, that you may proclaim the excellencies of Him who called you out of darkness into His marvelous light" (1 Peter 2:9).

God Himself, awareness of what He is like, what He has done, what He is doing and will do for us, is the very best and most powerful motivation that we can have for sharing Christ with others.

People-oriented motivation. Whenever we focus on God and His love we are soon directed to other people. When our grateful, loving faith makes us want to do something for Him, God says, "This pleases Me very much, but I don't really need anything. Everything is already Mine. However, other people need a lot. Above all, they need to know Me and what Jesus has done for them. Nothing will make Me happier, nothing will mean more to Me, than if you introduce them to Jesus. There are other ways to please Me, but this is at the top of the list."

People have all kinds of other needs, which also deserve our attention. Another chapter will address the importance of helping with those needs and explains how doing that can support our witness to them. However, we must give priority to their most urgent and basic need for God, their Savior. That does not mean that we always try to meet that need before we attend to their other needs. Actually, the opposite is often the case, as Jesus' own example demonstrates. He often began by healing or feeding and then followed that with preaching the Gospel. But He was always clear, as we must be, that their primary and most critical need was to be saved by knowing and trusting in Him.

Other priceless benefits and advantages accompany saving faith in Jesus. When we offer Him to others, we are offering all those as well. It is encouraging and motivating to realize what a huge favor we are doing others when we witness to them. We are aware of these blessings and are often reminded of them in preaching and teaching. They are so familiar that we may overlook their awesomeness. Those who receive our witness to Jesus receive with Him:

- the offer of God's complete, inexhaustible, unconditional love;
- total forgiveness for everything wrong in their heart and life;
- adoption into God's family, the Church;
- God's personal involvement in every aspect of this life in ways that make the best that happens even better, and even the worst a blessing;

- God's comfort and support in sorrow and trouble and hope in the face of death;
- at life's end, God's gracious welcome to unimaginable joy and peace with Him and all who have lived and died trusting in Jesus.

The enormity and value of these benefits can give us the will we need for Christian witness.

Self-fulfilling motivation. We do not share Christ primarily out of self-interest but out of love for God and other people. However, there are aspects of the witness experience that are richly rewarding, and it is encouraging to be aware of them. To be God's instrument in giving His supreme gift to those who need it is the most important service that a Christian can render. There is no greater privilege than the opportunity to do this. In addition, it brings the deep satisfaction of knowing that one has done the right thing, carried out a mission that means more to God than anything else in the world, and renders a vital service to fellow human beings, one that will make an eternal difference to them. We attain our highest potential as human beings when we introduce others to their Savior. No other achievement or gift gets close to it.

A conspicuous part of the motivation of New Testament witnesses was the natural delight of bringing Good News to others. This is not hard to understand. We enjoy bringing joy and hope to others, and the Gospel has that effect on those who accept it. Paul, for example, gloried in the privilege of serving as Christ's spokesman. He was proud of his ministry and regarded it as a gift of God's grace (Romans 15:15–17). His was the delightful task of spreading the fragrance of the knowledge of Christ everywhere (2 Corinthians 2:14). He was an ambassador of the Most High God (2 Corinthians 5:20). As such, he distributed the unsearchable riches of Christ to the Gentiles and revealed mysteries hidden for ages (Ephesians 3:8–9). Paul never ceased being amazed that he, the chief of sinners, had been granted the incredible privilege and opportunity not only to be saved by the Gospel but also to transmit it to others (1 Timothy 1:15–16). Every Christian witness can feel the same way.

Christian maturity consists of moving from lower to higher motivations. All three forms of motivation listed above are valid. We need to be aware of them and ready to respond to them. However, it is essential to observe priorities. Our best and most compelling reason for sharing Christ is that we want to please and honor God. We learn from Him that one of the best ways to do that is to help people, especially by offering them the salvation that He provided at so great a cost. An attractive by-product of pleasing God and helping people with our witness is that it brings a level of personal fulfillment unavailable in any other way.

Valid though it may be, self-fulfillment is the lowest level of motivation. Our sinful nature would like to keep us at this lowest level. As we experience some success, witnessing can degenerate into an ego trip, which we make primarily for ourselves. If and when this happens, the Holy Spirit is there to lead us through repentance and forgiveness to a better attitude. He will enable us to move from self-interest to love for God and for people. These are our best reasons for sharing Christ.

Practice

1. Identify a specific person with whom you have frequent contact who needs to know the Lord or know Him better. When you are with that person, or even thinking about him or her, reflect on the reasons why you can and should speak up. Why is this so important to God? To that person? To yourself? Note and record your reaction in your journal.

2. Your new neighbor, Sandra, is middle-aged, divorced, tense, and worldly in her attitudes and behavior as far as you can tell. She is cordial but distant. Over the back fence, in what had been a superficial chat, she dropped her guard a bit and revealed some of her bitterness and anxiety. Because you do not know her well, and because she has been distant, you hesitate to probe or say much. What can you tell *yourself* in order to generate proper motivation? Record your thoughts in your journal.

3 Transformation

Becoming Magnetically Christian

The Lord has an astonishing method of attracting attention to Himself and creating interest in what He has to offer. He introduces people to you and others like you who know Him, trust Him, and have come under His influence. He is confident that through you they will experience something of His love and strength, and that they will sense some of the joy and hope that He gives those who believe in Him. Just imagine—in order to make a good impression on others, to give them a sample of what to expect from Him, the Lord arranges for them to meet you.

Does this seem intimidating, even outrageous? Does it seem to put unbearable pressure on you? "Who am I to represent Jesus Christ? Who am I to serve as an example of what He is like? I am flawed, imperfect, and sinful. There is little or no similarity between us. Instead of drawing people to Him, I probably drive them away. Many people who will have nothing to do with Jesus blame it on the hypocrisy of Christians who do not live what they profess. Those who remind people of Jesus are rare. I just cannot think of myself as one of them."

In some respects, this is an appropriate reaction. We are sinful and seriously unlike our Savior. However, we cannot stop there. He has done something about that, and so can we. He has given us the potential to grow in our resemblance to Him, and we can realize that potential more and more. It is vital that this happens because it is a crucial part of His plan. To be more effective witnesses, we can and must become magnetically Christian. It is God's strategy to draw people to Himself through qualities and actions of believers. These qualities and actions, too, communicate Christ.

A. Transformed Attitudes and Behaviors Also Communicate Christ

We communicate Christ most clearly and completely when the witness of our lives is combined with the witness of our words. This is a subject that we will fully address later. Jesus revealed Himself and His mission through both word and deed, and so must we.

The transformed Christian life prepares for and supports spoken witness. Nothing does more to open someone to information about Jesus and to an invitation to believe than knowing someone who is being changed for the better under His influence. Not perfection but improvement, and the obvious and joyful intention to keep improving, are what awaken interest in the One who has made this transformation possible. The high claims that we make about our Savior gain credibility and are taken more seriously when His presence and influence are evident in our lives. Jesus says, "You are the light of the world. . . . Let your light shine before others, so that they may see your good works and give glory to your Father who is in heaven" (Matthew 5:14, 16). In other words, be the kind of person that reminds people of God and helps them to appreciate Him.

The apostle Peter is very explicit about the Christian life and suggests the effect upon unbelievers. After encouraging believers to be loving, compassionate, and cooperative with one another, he goes on to explain how they should react even to those who abuse and persecute them. Like Jesus, they are not to retaliate in any way to those who wrong them, or even be afraid of them. Rather, they should use their suffering as an opportunity to bring honor to Christ. This encouragement leads up to a very important point: "in your hearts honor Christ the Lord as holy, always being prepared to make a defense to anyone who asks you for a reason for the hope that is in you; yet do it with gentleness and respect, having a good conscience" (1 Peter 3:15–16). He is telling us that if we respond to others, even enemies, in a Christlike way, we are going to raise questions in their minds. We will make them want to know how and why we can be that way. That opens the door to a clear testimony to Jesus.

Transformed Christian lives say that God is real and that He makes a significant difference in human lives. Christlike behavior reveals that God is incredibly loving and forgiving, that He is deeply interested in us, and that He provides remarkable strength and confidence to those who trust in Him. In those whose potential for godly change is being realized, others see enviable joy and peace and purpose and hope. This happens not only with heroic martyrs but also with ordinary Christians with all their limitations and flaws. In His own wonderful way, God helps us to rise above our lingering sinfulness and to reflect some of His own winsome characteristics. He promises to do this, and He keeps that promise.

B. Believing That God Will Actually Transform Us

The prospect of growing in our resemblance to Jesus seems almost too good to be true. After all, we know what we are really like. Every day we face our weakness and failures. Even with the best of intentions we often fall short of what God expects and what we sincerely want to change. And, to our shame, too much of the time we knowingly resist God's will and lack even the desire to improve. So how can we seriously expect this important transformation to happen? All our experience seems to make change toward Christlikeness a delusion.

St. Paul addresses this skepticism very directly. He assures us that (*emphasis added*) we are "*predestined* to be conformed to the image of [God's] Son" (Romans 8:29). And that refers to a present reality, not just to our eternal future. That is made clear in another passage: "We . . . are *being transformed* into the same image from one degree of glory to another" (2 Corinthians 3:18). Furthermore, Paul refers to this change as an accomplished fact. After directing believers to get rid of a number of other sinful behaviors, he adds these challenging words: "Do not lie to one another, seeing that *you have put off the old self with its practices and have put on the new self,* which is being renewed in knowledge after the image of its creator" (Colossians 3:9). Through the work of Christ and the Holy Spirit, our sinful impulses and habits (old self) have become something that we can begin to discard like soiled clothing and replace with Christlike attitudes and actions (new self).

What Paul describes is not a sudden, immediate experience, but a process of growth and improvement. The fact that it is a work in progress explains why our Christlikeness is still only partial and often obscured by sin. However, it also tells us we have the potential and the opportunity for continued improvement. We have His word for it. We can count on it. We can believe that God is doing this in us and that He can do it more and more.

The Importance of Our Transformed Lives

These changes please and honor God. He wants us to become like His Son and has made it possible. Consequently, when His thoughts and feelings and responses are increasingly our own, He is delighted the way a parent is pleased when his child begins to reflect some of his good characteristics, or the way a teacher or coach observes their influences in their young charges. The reason that Christlike transformation means so much to God is that this is the way we were meant to be and because He has invested so much in making this possible. We matter to Him, more than we can imagine. He is profoundly disturbed by all that has gone wrong with us. We are the crown of His creation. Nothing means more to Him than making us right again. He and all the hosts of heaven celebrate our progress.

Unbelievers need to see our transformed lives. Many forces in our culture are working to mute or discredit the Gospel. Prevailing views in contemporary education and media try to explain our world and its creatures, including humans, and the entire universe without reference to God. Psychology and sociology interpret individual and group behavior in completely naturalistic terms. The spiritual dimension is ignored or even denied. These factors seem to make God unnecessary. Everything can be explained without Him, or so it seems. God and the saving sacrifice of His Son seem strange, out of step with the times, ridiculous.

That is, until the unbeliever experiences someone with strong, living, active faith, on whom Jesus has made a deep impression, someone who is noticeably Christlike in thought and action. Unbelievers can meet the living God in the person of a transformed believer. Theories that dismiss the reality of God somehow seem less convincing, and the possibility of a loving and forgiving God seems more inviting. The magnetism of God touches people through contact with Christians who have been changed in heart and life through their faith relationship with Jesus. Until that happens, unbelievers may remain perfectly comfortable in their detachment from or even hostility toward God. The difference in the Christian does not have to be complete or heroic. It just has to be unexpected and natural.

There was a time when I was without a paycheck for several months and urgently needed temporary employment. The country was in an economic downturn and jobs were scarce, but I finally found one in a factory. It was rough work done by rough men. They knew I was a Christian and a pastor and accepted the fact that, though cordial and friendly, I did not adopt their profane and obscene language or join in their lunchtime conversations dominated by dirty jokes. I did not criticize them for these behaviors. I simply acted differently.

However, there was one worker who seemed to hate me for this. For several weeks he carried on a campaign of taunting ridicule about my vocation and Christian values. With unusual (for me) patience and calm I just put up with it. I did not retaliate or answer back. I treated him as if he had not said these things. Then the unexpected happened. One day he came and sat down beside me while I was eating my lunch. He apologized for the way he had been treating me and poured out a long confession of sin. He had once been a Christian but had run away from the Lord and had been living a sinful life. Could I help him get right with God and turn his life around?

I report this not to brag about how I cracked a hard case, because that is not what happened. I had not even considered the possibility of getting through to him. I was simply trying to survive his abuse in a Christian way. But in that modest example of Christian faithfulness and love he saw something of the Savior whom he had abandoned and was moved to try to come back to Him. What a uniquely rewarding experience it was to become his guide on that journey. What he saw and experienced in me was nothing spectacular, but it was something that he needed, and that led to an enormous and eternal difference. The magnetic potential of simple Christian example is awesome.

This process of transformation that makes us begin to resemble Jesus is also good for us. It reverses some of the damage done by sin. It involves the exercise of the will and the development of new attitudes and habits. It does for us spiritually what an effective program of physical fitness does for our bodies. We become healthier, happier people, more in control of our lives, more fulfilled in our relationships. We have a clearer sense of purpose and are able to carry out that purpose more confidently. We become stronger and tougher in the face of hardship and more ready and willing to do what God expects. We have every reason to welcome gratefully everything that God does to transform us into more magnetically Christian people.

C. How God Works to Transform Us into Magnetic Christian People

It all begins with forgiveness through the sacrifice of His Son. What keeps us from being more like Jesus is our sinfulness and the guilt that it brings. Guilt makes us feel distant from God. It distracts us from His influence. It dwells on our failures and disempowers us. But God dispels our guilt, removes it from His record and from our conscience by applying what Jesus did and endured for us by His life, death, and resurrection. After pointing to our record of wrongdoing and neglect and the charges that stand against us with their terrifying consequences, God announces with loving authority, "But this has all been taken care of by your Savior. The charges and their consequences are dropped. You are pardoned. Your guilt no longer exists. It has been deleted from your record and cannot be retrieved. Neither your own conscience nor any other accuser has the right to bring it up." With a clean record and a conscience at rest we are ready to resume transformation.

The next step of our transformation is liberation. God is never satisfied only to remove the guilt of our sinfulness. He also insists on counteracting its power. He does this through His Holy Spirit, who always accompanies God's word of forgiveness. Forgiveness and the Holy Spirit always come together; you cannot have one without the other. There is great encouragement in this truth. It overcomes a defeatist attitude toward the impulses that have let us fail. It tells us that we do not have to yield to them, because we have the living power of the Holy Spirit with which to resist. When Jesus forgave the woman caught in the act of adultery, He added, "Go, and from now on sin no more" (John 8:11). He can say this with all seriousness because, with His pardon, He always also provides the power to break free from Satan and the sinful nature, which try to control us.

Having forgiven and freed us, the Spirit proceeds to restore us to Christlikeness. He creates a new person within us, a new self that begins to combat the sinful nature and exert God's own influence upon others. The Spirit deepens and strengthens faith, making us more aware of God and drawing us closer to Him. We begin to think and feel and act more like Jesus. We *want* to be like Him because the Spirit affects our will in that way. In the opportunities and challenges of life, "What would Jesus do?" becomes more than a pious platitude. It provides meaningful guidance as we decide what to do. We can and should try to live in a Christlike way, expressing His own selfless and sacrificial love and exhibiting His willing obedience to His Father. This is not something that we draw out of our own resources but rather from those provided by the Holy Spirit. Through that kind of personality and behavioral change, others see Jesus and are drawn to Him. His magnetism reaches out through us, preparing for and supporting our witness.

D. Opportunities for Demonstrating Christlikeness

Opportunities to demonstrate our Christlikeness are abundant. We will recognize them if we look at other people through the eyes of God and respond to them with the heart of God. The suggestions that follow are a few specifics of what Christlike love might look like: Notice people. Treat them as if they matter; they do! Be sensitive to their feelings. Be appreciative of the service that they render. Ask for small favors. Lend a helping hand without being asked. Be polite and considerate. Be compassionate and supportive when others are struggling. People in all kinds of situations deserve such treatment. Look into the faces of those who serve you for clues about what is going on in their lives—the cashier, the restaurant server, the repairperson. Do you see tension, fatigue, joy, and seriousness about their task? By just the right comment or inquiry or facial expression, you can let them know that you sense what they are experiencing. Relate to them as persons, not just as machines that do something that you need.

Reactions to such treatment can be astonishing. It was the end of a busy and trying day at the clinic. The nurse came into the waiting room with a scowl on her face and a set jaw because I wanted to discuss a serious and disappointing mistake that she may have made with a prescription. I sensed her need for understanding, and began by assuring her that my concern was for our relationship and not for attaching blame. She and her doctor are very important to me and I want to have confidence in them. Would she just explain what happened?

As she did, it became very clear that it was not her but the pharmacy that had let me down. She had responded to my emergency request for medication promptly and conscientiously. When I assured her that I believed her and apologized for thinking that it may have been carelessness on her part, she shed tears of joy and hugged me. In the course of future visits to the clinic I may have a good opportunity to say something about Jesus. If I do, I believe that this interaction will help to open the door. Something as simple as this can prepare for and support witness to Jesus.

Practice

Every day, in your family, at work or school, and out in the community you have opportunities to reflect the reality and love of God, to be magnetically Christian, to give others a glimpse of their Savior.

© shutterstock.com/Karelias

1. Intentionally watch for such opportunities. How could you respond in a way that shows some of Jesus' own interest and concern for them as persons?
2. Record these experiences in your journal for your personal growth and for sharing.

4
Clarification

Knowing What to Say

Up to this point we have been concentrating on preparation for spoken witness, and this preparation is essential. If we do not deal with our fears, become more motivated, and actually live what we believe, our words about Jesus will not receive the hearing that they deserve. And, in fact, we may not even get around to saying something. Frightened, halfhearted, or unspoken witness does not evoke interest in Jesus or longing to know Him better.

However, as important as the preliminaries are—confidence, motivation, and Christlike living—complete Christian witness has not taken place until they are joined to the Gospel message. Eventually, the witness must either say something personally or somehow connect another to the Gospel. It is through that message, that Word about who Jesus is, what He has done, and what He means to us, that hearts are opened, minds are changed, and eternal hope is born. For that Word is alive with the Holy Spirit. He is the one who creates faith. He convinces people of their sinfulness and desperate need for Jesus and then enables them to say YES to all that He is, does, and offers.

We often hesitate to speak up because we do not know what to say. We imagine that it may be better to say nothing about Jesus than to say something wrong, confusing, or irrelevant to the hearer. It is important to say what builds up others and meets their needs (Ephesians 4:29), and we should be concerned about that. However, we cannot let that concern keep us silent. Rather, we need to acquire a clear and complete grasp of what the message is that we are to convey. And we need to know how to relate that to the needs and situation of our hearer. That is our agenda in this chapter.

A. Witness Is a Personal and Positive Form of Communication

Christian witness is a distinctive type of human communication, personal and not just a statement of fact. Christian witness is me saying what I have seen, heard, or experienced. It is like the sworn comments of someone who saw an accident or crime. It is saying, "I was there and this is what happened." The apostle John insists that what he says and writes about Jesus is based on what he saw, heard, and touched (1 John 1:1). Similarly, the apostle Peter explains that he and the other followers of Jesus did not make up these remarkable events that they reported, but were eyewitnesses (2 Peter 1:16). The testimony of reliable eyewitnesses is weighty and convincing.

Although we cannot claim to be eyewitnesses of Jesus, we are in a position to speak from credible personal experience. We can say we know that Jesus is real and that He does what He claims because He has touched our hearts and lives and made a huge difference. Through His Holy Spirit He has convinced us that we need forgiveness and that we can have it through His suffering and death. This happened through the testimony of those who were eyewitnesses as recorded in the Bible. What we received through their scriptural witness was not just information about Jesus but His personal presence conveyed by the Spirit. He promised that those who learned to know Him through the eyewitnesses would receive the same blessings of faith and forgiveness that they did (John 20:19–31). Although we have not seen Him with our eyes, we do know Him personally, and He has helped us in ways that no one else could. The subject is Jesus, but it is delivered in the first person from the perspective of that kind of experience.

Because it is about personal conviction and experience, your witness is not controversial or debatable. Better than anyone else, you know what you believe, what you have been through, and what it means to you. Someone else might doubt your credibility or sanity. They might regard you as deluded and may not want any part of it, but they cannot possibly know your deepest thoughts and feelings the way you do. Except for God Himself, you are the best authority on yourself. No one has any reason to debate or disagree with that aspect of what you say. However, the message is not all about you. As will be seen below, it is all about Jesus.

Your part is to share Jesus with others in a way that says, "I know that this is all true because I have put it to the test in my own heart and life, and it works!" Your witness to Jesus is your personal recommendation based on your positive and convincing experience. It is like sharing your opinion of a physician who has successfully treated a frightening illness or a vacation destination that was extraordinarily satisfying.

At its best, Christian witness is shaped by input from the hearers. This begins most naturally with inquiry about work, family, and other matters that are not controversial. There will be more about this below and in the next chapter. Here it is important to note that witness is usually most effective as part of a conversation. People are usually interested in talking about themselves. Listening to them carefully and with interest can help you to understand them and shape your comments to them in a fitting way. It can also prepare them to listen.

If and when you are able to bring the conversation to Jesus and what He has done for them, you will want to invite them to respond. What do you think about this? How do you feel about that? Questions such as these can lead to even deeper discussion or at least alert you to issues that need to be considered. This can be done in a sensitive and winsome way. It is an invitation that may be accepted or declined, and the witness will be gracious either way. More often than not, they will accept the opportunity. People are ordinarily far more willing to take seriously a personal testimony that is part of a conversation than they are a scripted message.

B. Some Easy Transitions

This is a point at which the net of fear (chapter 1) tries to enclose us and seal our lips. After some casual conversation about other things, how do we get into a discussion about Jesus in a way that is natural and unforced? Too often we just cannot think of a way to do it, and so we do nothing. Ironically, this may seem most difficult **with people whom we know rather well** but with whom, for one reason or another, we have never talked about the all-important subject of Jesus and their salvation. **This can be surprisingly easy to do.** In this kind of a personal relationship, we can be right up front: "I would like to change the subject. We have known each other for quite a while and talked about all kinds of things. For a long time I have wanted to talk with you about something that is very important to me. It's Jesus. Tell me what you know about Him. Has He ever been important to you?" Friends and acquaintances can talk to one another like this. In most cases, the conversation will develop to the point that you will be able to say what you know about Him and what He means to you. If the person does not want the conversation to take that turn, do not take this as a final negative. Rather, wait and pray for a better opportunity.

Short-term contacts are different, sometimes even easier. Many people are more comfortable discussing such things with strangers than with family or friends. How can you break the conversational ice with the person sitting next to you on an airplane or in a waiting room? The simplest and yet most interesting approach that I know was developed by a Russian pastor who was a relatively new Christian. In that type of situation, after casual words about weather, travel, or whatever, he simply asks, "Do you know Jesus?" Most reply in the negative. Then he follows with, "Would you like to know Him?" And most say, "Yes!" This transition may need to be adapted in North America to, "*How well* do you know Jesus?" Or simply, "Tell me about your faith."

Another approach has worked well for one of my sisters. Before leaving on a flight, Barbara prays to be placed next to someone who needs Jesus. Then, toward the end of the flight, so as not to make the person feel trapped, if the passenger next to her is not engrossed in reading or conversation with someone else, Barbara says, "I like to pray for the person next to me. Is that all right?" If it is, she adds: "Is there anything in particular that you want me to pray for?" Most of these simple requests evoke positive responses and provide the opportunity to turn someone's thoughts toward the Lord. Barbara recalls, "I asked a Muslim lady to share her beliefs about Jesus, and I explained mine. She was grateful for my prayers and introduced me to her Christian husband in a very enthusiastic way. I suggested that she attend church with him where she could hear more about her Savior."

There are many other possibilities. After mentioning something in your life related to church, you might ask, "What is your church background?" Then follow up with: "Is it important to you? Was it ever?" Most people have had an experience with the church and do not mind talking about it. Think of this as an opening point only. Do not let the conversation remain centered on the church. Often people have complaints and criticisms about the church, and we are inclined to stand up for it. Instead, it is better to respond with something like, "You know, the issue is not the church. It's Jesus. What do you think about Him?" As that conversation develops, you will have the opportunity to say that He is very important to you and why. Once the centrality of Jesus has been established, you can return to the subject of the church. "What makes the church so important to me is that this is where I meet Jesus. He is there in person among His people through His Word," would be a way to express that, along with encouragement to attend worship.

This leads to other opportunities that you have to put others in touch with Jesus after you have introduced them to Him. You might recommend powerful films such as *The Nativity*, *Jesus*, and *The Passion of the Christ*. If someone appreciates fine music, suggest that they listen to a recording of Handel's "Messiah." At Christmas and Easter some large churches offer quality, biblically-sound dramatic productions about the life and work of Jesus. In addition, there are books about Jesus and believers that put the message in interesting and meaningful terms. These can be effective reinforcement of our personal witnessing.

Often, conversations turn to all that is wrong in the world, all the things that hurt or threaten us. When that happens, we have an opportunity to say something relevant and encouraging. "No matter how bad things get for me personally or for the world, I have hope. I know that for me, and everyone who trusts in Jesus, the final outcome will be marvelous. And in the meantime, He will be with me and help me through trouble, and turn the worst of it into a blessing."

Other examples could be given. The point of all of them is that God does give us opportunities, even in brief contacts, to share Christ confidently in ways that can connect with the lives and concerns of people. Like my sister Barbara, we can pray for such opportunities and take advantage of them gratefully.

C. The Good News: Christ Is the Solution to Our Most Serious Problems

There are various ways to express that Christ is the solution. It is most helpful and meaningful to use terms that speak to the needs and situation of the hearer. For example, those who reveal recognition and regret over wrongdoing are ready to hear that **Christ paid for our guilt** with His own blood and death. Those who are in pain need to know that Christ knows what we are going through and will support us in our suffering. Christ **has suffered for us,** so that we can look forward to a life in which there will be none. Those who are lonely need to know that Christ empathizes with them, **has experienced and overcome the worst kind of loneliness**—separation from God, and will fill the void with His own presence. Those addicted to any evil substance or behavior need assurance of **Christ's liberating victory over forces that hold us in bondage.** People worried about death can find hope in knowing that by His death and resurrection **Christ has made a way for us through death to a life that never ends.** The Bible is rich with vivid language that conveys the Good News to the heart.

We do have something to say about Jesus, something very specific that everyone needs to hear. Essentially, Christian witness is expressing in our own words and way what He has done for us, what He means to us, why we want to recommend Him to others. It does not have to be fancy or even fluent, just a clear and sincere sharing of what is in your heart about the One who loved us and gave Himself for us.

D. A Witness Experience

I was tired after a demanding day and on my way by air to another. I really hoped to just withdraw into myself and recharge for what was ahead. The man sitting next to me had other ideas. To initiate the conversation, he asked about my destination and my work, and I gave him a short answer. This is what followed:

"Oh, religion. I don't have any use for organized religion. I'm going to make up my own."

"That's interesting. How did you arrive at that decision?" I replied.

"What they say in churches doesn't make any sense. Three persons but only one God? Who can figure that out?" was his answer.

My comment was, "It doesn't surprise me that God is more complicated than I am."

He was thinking about that when I asked, "When was the last time you were in church?"

With an astonished look on his face he said, "Christmas Eve."

"What happened?"

His eyes grew wide as he answered, "I cried through the whole thing."

From there I went on to say that apparently he had not left it all behind and that it still meant something to him. He agreed but complained about some bad experiences he had had at church. I urged him not to let that get in the way, but to go to worship expecting to meet God. He wants you to know how much you matter to Him, how much His Son went through for you. Jesus did not stay safe in His mother's arms as we think of Him at Christmas. He grew up to face terrible rejection, pain, and death to make up for everything that is wrong in our hearts and lives. He wants you to have the benefit of all this and to be close to Him. Are you going to accept it?

The man sitting next to me was moved, said our conversation was important to him, wanted to meet again and talk further. It so happened that we were staying at the same hotel, so the possibilities looked promising. However, I was not able to reach him, and we had failed to exchange business cards so there could be no further contact. Yet it was a memorable experience of witness that connected, and hopefully made a lasting difference.

Practice

1. Write at least one paragraph in which you explain what Jesus means to you.
2. In your own words, express your Christian witness in a real or imaginary conversation. You may base it on one of the themes under C above.
3. Record it in your journal.

5
Communication

Getting the Message Across

With regard to witnessing, you have probably heard it said that it is our job to deliver the message and that the results are up to God. Only He can awaken or strengthen faith. This, of course, is correct. *But what does it mean to deliver the message?* Does it mean that as long as we get the words on paper and into someone's hands we have done our job? Or as long as we have sounded the words in someone's hearing we have accomplished our assignment as Christian witnesses? Or is there more to our assignment?

A. The Role of Persuasion

Paul adds a vital dimension, "Therefore, knowing the fear of the Lord, we persuade others" (2 Corinthians 5:11). In Acts 18:4 we are told, "[Paul] reasoned in the synagogue every Sabbath, and tried to persuade Jews and Greeks." These references indicate that there is a place for persuasion, perhaps even a responsibility to be persuasive, when sharing Christ with others. But what is that place? Paul makes it clear elsewhere that it is the Holy Spirit who enables people to say that Jesus is their Lord (1 Corinthians 12:3). If that is the case, what is our persuasion supposed to do?

Whenever the Gospel is presented, the role of persuasion is to secure the attention of hearers and encourage them to take it seriously. We cannot persuade them to believe, but we can try to persuade them to listen and consider what is said. In that respect, persuasive comments about Jesus have an effect similar to that of a transformed Christian life. They create interest in and openness to the message. They carry the message through the ears and eyes and brain into the heart where the Holy Spirit works faith. A word of witness to which no one pays attention is not going to benefit anyone. Witnessing is communication.

Effective witnessing is that which actually gets through to the hearer in a way that leads to reflection and evaluation.

B. What Makes Witnessing Persuasive?

The attitude of the witness is crucial. If we obviously value Christ highly and feel privileged to tell about Him, this invites attention. Once I was in a showroom full of new cars. I was looking at one with interest when a salesman approached me. I had already explained to him that I was not in the market for a new car and he accepted that. But he walked up to the one I was looking at, actually caressed it lovingly, and said, "Isn't it beautiful!" That's all he said, and he was sincere. I did not buy that car, but shortly afterward returned and purchased another. That salesman and his manner not only created confidence but also left a lasting impression on me. He did get my attention. He made me realize that we can do something like this when we share Christ with others. By our attitude toward Him, as well as our words, we can say, "Isn't He wonderful!"

A message that is clear, interesting, and expressed in a natural way encourages attentive consideration. Perhaps most important, if what we say addresses *their* questions and felt needs, they will want to listen. In order to do that, we have to find out what they are. An essential aspect of effective communication is knowing something about the person to whom we are witnessing.

A sense of urgency can stimulate interest. If we sincerely believe that the message about Jesus is of vital importance to the hearer, there will be some urgency in our manner. If I really believe that someone is walking into a trap or away from a golden opportunity, my warning or plea will not be matter-of-fact. The expression on my face, the tone of my voice, and my choice of words will all say: *This you have to hear! You can't afford not to hear it.* Even if I deliberately restrained myself and delivered the message calmly, it would convey urgency. A sense of urgency is a valuable tool of witness, but one that must be used sparingly and carefully to avoid an impression of fanaticism. To prepare to use a sense of urgency, if it should be called for, just consider before saying anything how important it is for that person to know Jesus or to know Him better. Imagine the benefits if he did and the loss if he didn't.

C. Basics of Communication

Because witnessing about Jesus is a process of communication, it is helpful to keep in mind what this process involves. Essentially, communication consists of two inseparable actions. It begins when someone transmits a message and is completed when another actually receives the message. So the formula may be expressed: **transmission (speaking) + reception (listening) = communication**. Neither transmission nor reception by itself is communication. Chapter 4 devoted attention to the importance of shaping your witness by input from the hearer and offered suggestions and examples for inviting that input. Now we are going to explore some problems and possibilities in the listening or reception aspect of communication.

Test for reception. Early in your conversation, try to determine if the other person is actually listening and with what effect. Facial expression and body language tell a lot. Is he puzzled or interested, uncomfortable or relaxed? At some point, before you go too far, it may be helpful to invite a verbal response. "Is this new to you? How do you feel about it? Did I make myself clear?" Questions like these should be asked in a way that indicates genuine interest in the other person and in your effectiveness as a communicator. You do not want to put him or her on the spot.

If others express discomfort, verbally or otherwise, respect that. Explain (with a touch of urgency) that you would like to say more because you know how important it is, but also want to be sensitive to their feelings. Would they mind saying what is causing discomfort and why? It might be possible to dispel their discomfort about that element or set it aside at least temporarily without nullifying your witness. Or it might suggest a different approach another time. There are elements in the Christian message that are very unflattering, but must be said and received. However, they will be effective only if the hearer is ready for them. In any case, sensitive regard for the other person can only help good listening.

Hidden messages. People do not always mean what they say or say what they mean. In fact, what they mean down deep may be the exact opposite of what they are saying or acting out. We must keep that in mind and act accordingly. Remember Billy (chapter 2)? He seemed to have no interest in the Lord or His Word and only liked to cause trouble. But inwardly he had a heart for sharing Jesus. The young man in the factory (chapter 3) spoke and acted as if he hated the Lord and everyone associated with Him, but deep down wanted to get right with God. The passenger next to me in the airplane (chapter 4) sounded as if he wanted to discuss the doctrine of the Trinity or the unpleasantness of church life, but in fact had a longing to be close to God. People who seem negative or even hostile to Jesus and what He stands for may be conflicted and struggling with contrary feelings. If they were completely confident and comfortable in their unbelief, they would not have the need to react so emphatically. Sometimes you can probe or even challenge, as I did to the airplane passenger. With others, your Christian example might break through their hard shell. In still other cases, God may intervene in their lives in a way that makes them aware of their desperate need for Him. Because there may be hidden messages in negative responses to our witness, it is important to try to keep the door open. Perhaps the simplest way to do this is simply to say, "If you change your mind, be sure to let me know."

Recognizing and responding to hidden messages. Not all comments or actions contain hidden messages. However, they are common, and when witnessing we will want to be alert for them. Especially when someone seems very negative about the Lord or the church, ask yourself, does this person really feel that way, or is that a cover for something else? Do not argue or disagree. Rather, acknowledge the negative feelings calmly and with interest. "I can see that you feel very strongly about this. I would be very interested to know how you came to feel this way." This could encourage full disclosure, including the real reason, if followed up carefully. After the other person has finished explaining, you might respond, "Thanks very much. That really helps me to understand where you are coming from. Just to be sure that I heard you correctly, is this what happened?" Summarize the explanation in your own words. Then add, "Did anything else enter into this?" This could demonstrate interest in and respect for the person's experience and feelings and encourage further conversation. It could also encourage willingness to hear how you arrived at your convictions.

Unblocking reception. When our witness does not get across, is not received by another, it is often because we have failed to listen or to have invited feedback. We may have been so preoccupied with what we wanted to say that we squelched the kind of response that would have enabled us to say it most effectively. In other words, our focus on transmission interfered with reception. Effective personal transmission of the Gospel grows out of effective listening.

Being an effective listener. This begins with setting aside our own fears, needs, and troubles and focusing on the other person. This cannot be faked. It is a matter of genuinely caring about the other person, what is going on in their hearts and lives, and tuning in to their feelings and needs. This is what God's love is like and what God's love wants to do through us. This is not a sentimental feeling. It is an act of the will made possible by the Holy Spirit's influence within us. He enables us to look at others through God's eyes and respond to them with His heart. He not only tells us to be that way; He also provides the desire and the love to be that kind of listener. It involves noticing and trying to understand the reaction of the other person. It includes being sensitive to their feelings, behaviors, and attitudes, even when they cannot be approved. When this kind of listening takes place, a trusting relationship can develop, and the Christian can earn the right to be heard. Such a relationship provides excellent opportunities for expressing the Gospel in a way that speaks meaningfully to the hearer.

D. Leave the Door Open

No matter how earnestly and skillfully we try to communicate Christ, the process often breaks down. For various reasons, our hearers cannot or will not receive the saving message. The response we hoped and prayed for did not take place or even begin. They are so negative and seem so final about it that we may walk away disappointed, perhaps hurt and angry. That is a serious mistake, especially if they can sense this in us. We cannot help but care, but we do not have to despair. Only God knows everything that was going on in their hearts and minds. We may have made more progress than we realize. The way to leave an "unsuccessful" witnessing opportunity is with the hope expressed in the statement, "I'm glad we had a chance to talk. *If you change your mind, be sure to let me know.*" People do change their minds, and we always want to leave the door open.

Two women, one middle-aged and the other her adult daughter, both serious Christians and faithful worshipers, lingered at the church door after service with this request, "Pastor, we want you to try to talk to Dad about the Lord. He is a hard case."

An angry face met me at the front door. After I introduced myself, he snapped, "What are you doing here? I've thrown out better pastors than you already."

"Sorry you feel that way," I replied. "If you change your mind, be sure to let me know."

About six months later, mother and daughter had another request. "Dad is the hospital. He is dying of liver cancer, and he would like to see you."

I was at his hospital room almost immediately. His attitude had changed dramatically. His first words were an apology for the way he had treated me, which I was happy to accept. Then he continued, "Do you know what's happened to me?" I admitted that I did know about his terminal cancer. He said, "I'm scared." I told him that I could understand that. Then he raised the all-important question, "Is there any way you can help me get right with God before I die?"

In the two weeks he had left, I was able to introduce him to his Savior, receive his confession of sin and of faith, absolve him, and prepare him to receive the Lord's Supper. He died a grateful and hopeful believer. Despite his initially negative response, the time came when he was more than ready to go through the open door.

Practice

1. Imagine this conversation with Sandra:
   You. Did I see you at the Arlington Inn the other evening?
   Sandra. Friday, about six? Yes, I was there. I eat there a lot. I hate to cook.
   You. Their Friday Special is great. I don't see how they price it so low.
   Sandra. It's a bargain, all right. (Pause and a trace of emotion.) I also like the people.

2. What feelings or meanings may be indicated? How could you encourage her to share them?
3. How might the conversation develop toward mention of Jesus?
4. Record your thoughts in your journal.

6
Expectation

Cultivating a Positive Response

To a significant degree, the response of the listener is conditioned by the expectant attitude of the witness. If you expect your listener to be interested and positive about what you are saying, it will encourage him or her to be that way. Enthusiasm can be contagious. Optimism on your part can create openness and affirmation in your listener.

This expectancy cannot be faked, and it is not something that you can generate on your own. Although you can try to be expectant, the expectancy needed for witnessing is the gift and work of God in you. When you have that gift, it will be evident not only in your words but also on your face. Furthermore, that expectancy will affect your perception of the situation and the other person. It will enable you to recognize opportunities to share the Savior as they arise and to sense the readiness of the other person to hear it. Often we notice what we are expecting to encounter and fail to notice and respond to what we were not expecting. How can we obtain genuine expectancy? How does God prepare us to tell others about Jesus with sincere expectation, the kind that will provide opportunities and some level of success? God prepares His witnesses through:

A. Prayer

Previous chapters have included brief references to prayer and how it may be used in relation to witnessing. Here we will consider specifically how **God uses prayer to instill expectation**. Jesus gives us a wide-open invitation, "Whatever you ask in My name, this I will do. . . . If you ask Me anything in My name, I will do it" (John 14:13–14). To ask in His name means, first of all, trusting in Him as our Savior. It also means trusting that His will is better than ours. So, in effect, when we pray for something, it is with the understanding and confidence, that if necessary, He will revise our request to bring it into conformity with His will, answering in a different way or at a different time than we had requested. If we connect the entire process of witnessing with such prayer, we will have every reason to expect significant results.

We know that it is His will that we introduce others to Him: "You will be My witnesses" (Acts 1:8). We know that He wants others to believe and be saved. What is said of John the Baptist also applies to us. He was sent by God "as a witness . . . that all might believe through him" (John 1:7). So, when we pray that God would help us to share Jesus, we can be sure that this is in keeping with His will. We can be positive of a positive response to that request, and that should raise our expectations. We are not on our own in this venture. He is with us, working in and through us. He is personally involved in the situation and very eager for it to be a fruitful encounter.

What specifically should we pray for? First, at the beginning of the day we should ask God to bring us together with others who need to know Him or to know more about Him. In addition, we should ask Him to help us to be alert to the opportunities He provides for witness and then to help us be clear and winsome in what we say, as well as sensitive in listening and responding to what has been said. Since we know that He wants our witness communication to be effective, and we have prayed seriously about it, we can expect it to happen, look for it to happen, and enthusiastically make it happen.

Prayer for those to whom we witness is also extremely important. We can ask God to make them attentive and interested in what we say, and to prevent Satan from interfering with distraction or confusion. We can ask Him to move them to be open about themselves and their experience so that we will know how to relate His love and promises to them. We can ask that the Holy Spirit accompany our words, inviting and encouraging them to move toward Jesus in faith. We can ask God not to let them forget what they heard but remember and consider it. We can ask God to intervene in their lives in such a way that they will feel the need for Him and the salvation that they were offered. Is God willing to do such things for your hearers? Of course He is. You can expect it to happen. You can count on it to happen in one way or another, sooner or later. God loves to answer prayers like these.

Like many others, I have experienced **the difference that prayer makes in witnessing**. When I remember to pray this way, witness opportunities appear even in unlikely situations. People open their hearts unexpectedly. I feel comfortable and confident in what I am saying, and they respond surprisingly. When I forget to pray, which happens more often than it should because I am expecting less, less happens. God wants us to expect more to happen when we witness, and we have every reason to approach it with that attitude. Through His promises about prayer and through answers to prayers, He raises our expectations in a way that makes sharing our faith a positive, even an exciting, venture. Prayer is a very basic method that God uses to create lively expectation in His witnesses.

B. Faith

The living, personal, saving, and transforming faith of the witness also stimulates expectation. It gives credibility to what we say. Others can tell if what we offer them is something that we ourselves have and value. To use an inadequate example from the marketplace, we are not salespersons for Jesus and His salvation; we are satisfied customers. Furthermore, we are not simply trying to deliver information or peddle a product. Nor are we trying to win an argument. We are trying to introduce others to a person, a person whom they need desperately and whom they will love if they get to know Him. And we are the ones who can do this. We know Him personally and have experienced the difference that He makes, not only with hope for the life to come but also in this life. We know that He makes the best of this life even better, turns even the worst of life into a blessing, and assures us of a spectacular future when this life is over. Our conviction and confidence about Him based on personal experience can be contagious. We can expect it to help open the minds and hearts of our hearers.

Trust in God and the power of His Word also builds expectation in the witness. What we share in witnessing is not just our opinion or something that we made up. It is God's own Word. That Word is powerful. By His Word God created the entire universe as well as everything and everyone in it. By His Word God will pronounce judgment, either pardon or condemnation, on every human being. By His Word God will bring this world to an end and present His people with a new heaven and a new earth. God's Word is not just print on a page or sound in the air. It is living and powerful. It is God Himself creating, judging, rescuing, and communicating. Jesus is God's word in human flesh and form, revealing Himself in terms that we can understand, as one of us in every way except without sin. In Jesus, we meet God as He pours out His love for us most completely. In Jesus, God expresses His urgent and irrepressible desire to embrace us as His children and lavish us with blessings. When we tell people about Jesus, we are offering them all this and more. It is an appealing offer, one that, if it gets through, we can expect to evoke a positive response. Most important, we know that the Holy Spirit accompanies the offer, and this enables the hearer to accept it. Paul says, "I am not ashamed of the gospel, for it is the power of God for salvation to everyone who believes" (Romans 1:16). No wonder that we can realistically expect results when we share that Gospel.

C. Hope

No one is a hopeless case. People can and do change radically. Saul of Tarsus is a classic example. He was a fanatic enemy and persecutor of Christians. He was an intelligent, well-informed, tough-minded unbeliever. Christians were afraid to talk to him, but God had His way of getting through, and Saul became Paul, the first and greatest missionary of all times. As mentioned earlier, hostility to Christianity is often evidence of an internal struggle against a God-given impulse to believe. In other cases, the hardest shell of resistance to the Gospel can be shattered by a hard blow of adversity. People who seemed hopelessly anti-Christian sometimes have second thoughts when faced with great danger or imminent death. I have referred to several of my experiences with "hopeless" people who changed. God is the reason why people make these about-face changes in their attitude toward Him. Either directly, as in the case of Paul, or indirectly through health or relational or economic crises, or a Christian witness, God will bring people to the realization that they need Him.

It does not always happen, but it happens enough that we have reason to expect it. Every Christian who is serious about sharing Christ will **be alert for and responsive to any indication that a "hopeless" unbeliever may be reconsidering**. As was already mentioned, one such indication may be intense, even angry, hostility, which is sometimes a sign that the issue is not as well-settled as one might assume.

The protester wants to be negative but something inside makes this person feel differently, and he or she is struggling with that. How can we respond to that possible clue to change? If the person is in some kind of crisis, we can respond with interest and support—be a friend. Encourage discussion about what the this person is going through and how he or she feels. That conversation might well indicate a change. Be an empathetic friend. Accept the person's right to reject the Lord even as you wait for an opening to say something about Him. Continue to be friendly and compassionate even to those who never change. In the case of someone who is militantly hostile, at just the right time and in the right way you might say, "If you really feel that the Lord doesn't exist or that you have driven Him out of your heart and life, why are you still struggling with Him so angrily?" That might just make the person's heart harder, but it also might give him or her pause to think. Expect a "hopeless" unbeliever to change. You have nothing to lose, and what the unbeliever could gain is priceless.

Regard your witness as part of a larger effort to reach the "hopeless." You are not the only one through whom God can reach a "hopeless" unbeliever. He has many other people on His team who can contribute to His work of creating or strengthening faith. Your part may be only to begin the process or to move it along. In another case, God may use you to complete the process by receiving the person's confession of faith. You never know when you witness to someone what role you may be filling, so you are always looking for the opportunity for completion.

Although he had been a lifelong Christian, serious and active, Ray (not his real name) had turned away from the Lord and remained in unbelief for decades. Now he was terminally ill in a hospital more than a thousand miles away from family and friends. An earnest and tenacious friend had been encouraging him for many years in long-distance phone conversations about returning to the Lord, and he indicated that Ray was having second thoughts about his unbelief. Then, to my surprise, this friend suggested that I call Ray and try to help him move closer to the Lord. I protested that I had not talked to Ray for more than twenty years and my witness to him had not been at all effective. However, at the insistence of this friend, I made the call without much expectation or optimism. His response was astonishing.

I did not even have to bring up the subject of faith in Jesus. He launched into an account of his illness and how the imminence of death brought to mind all that he had known, believed, and shared with others. He confessed his unworthiness and the hope that he found in Jesus. I could hardly believe my ears and replied, "Ray, did I hear a clear confession of faith in Jesus as your Savior?" To which he replied, "Absolutely!" What did I contribute? Very little. His pastors and teachers early in life had introduced him to Jesus and nurtured him. His tenacious friend, and others, had done the vital work of continuing to remind him of his Savior and his need to return. I was given the high privilege of hearing his confession of faith, even though I did not explicitly invite him to do this. It was as St. Paul said, "I planted, Apollos watered, but God gave the growth" (1 Corinthians 3:6).

Always leave the door open, no matter how negative the response. This was already discussed in chapter 5. Here we need simply emphasize that "hopeless" unbelievers do sometimes come through that open door. There is good reason to hope and pray and witness and wait for the "hopeless" to do that. That is what my tenacious friend believed and acted upon with marvelous results. Whether our part in the process is minor or major, it is done in hope. Our final reply to a negative response should always be, *"If you change your mind, be sure to let me know."*

D. Love

Let concern for the well-being of the other be your dominant concern. Too often when we approach an opportunity to witness, we are wrapped up in ourselves. We are dominated by self-consciousness or uneasiness or fear of rejection. A sense of duty is what makes us do it, and we will be glad when it is over with so that we can get back into our comfort zone. Or, if we are skillful at debate, we might look at the other as an opponent with whom could win an argument. Instead, our attitude can and should be one of Christlike love. He had deep concern and compassion for those who are lost, pleaded with them, wept over them, and He did whatever it took to locate them and save them. Christ's focus was on them and what they needed, not on Himself. He could be tough on those who did not think they needed Him and His salvation and who opposed Him, but only to try to bring them to their senses. Anyone who was open to His message or to conversation was treated with sensitivity and respect.

Avoid anything that might be viewed as pressure or manipulation. These interfere with choice and invite resistance and resentment. Christian witness is an offer and an invitation, which include power from the Holy Spirit to accept. We urgently want others to say yes. We try to persuade them to seriously consider Jesus and what He has done for them. We hope and even expect a positive response. Persistence is appropriate. But we have no right or ability to force them. God will not do that, and He does not want us to attempt it. It is loveless, offensive, and counterproductive. Bribery, punishment, deceit, emotion, social pressure, and anything else that compromises the freedom of those to whom we witness are violations of love. Well-meaning Christians sometimes resort to these measures in connection with sharing their faith, but the Holy Spirit does not need or honor them.

Love for those who decline. As disappointing as it is when people are negative about Jesus, we respond with love. We respect their right to resist or reject our testimony because it is God-given. He does not want to force Himself on anyone. If there is to be a relationship between Him and people, He insists that it be willingly on their part. Through the message about Jesus the Holy Spirit enables, but does not force, people to believe. It requires a miracle by the Holy Spirit for them to believe, but they are able to refuse all by themselves. In addition, we should be friendly and compassionate with those who turn us down. If we are interested in them only because they are prospective believers, we are being phony and manipulative.

E. History

History is very encouraging about the power of Christian witness. Throughout the centuries, Christians have experienced the amazing potential of a Gospel witness to bring people to faith in Jesus. All kinds, including atheists, skeptics, and even enemies of Christ, have been turned into ardent, witnessing believers. Never in the long history of Christian missions has there been a people group in which no one believed after they were presented with adequate Christian witness. There are always some, if only a few. In our own time, millions have been converted, even in Muslim and Communist countries where it is illegal and dangerous to do so. God has promised that His Word will not return to Him empty but will accomplish what He wants it to do (Isaiah 55:11). And we know what that purpose is: "God our Savior . . . desires all people to be saved and to come to the knowledge of the truth" (1 Timothy 2:3–4). So, when we share the saving truth about Jesus, we can do so with high expectations.

Shared experience is encouraging. Christian witnesses need one another. Expectation and excitement about sharing Christ also grow out of being with and hearing the stories of others who actively witness. Such encouragement and support are vital. This suggests that in every congregation there should be a group seriously committed to this purpose. Until and unless that happens, encouragement and support can be found in workshops and conferences offered by other congregations or the church body. To grow attitudes and skills necessary for effective witnessing, seek out other like-minded Christians. Pray that God will lead you to just the right individual or group.

There is no substitute for action. No matter how much we read or hear about sharing our faith, we will not become confidently expectant and truly effective unless we actually do it. A famous author was asked to speak to a group of advanced university students of literature and composition and give them some suggestions about how to become successful writers. After a long and elegant introduction by the presiding official, he came to the podium and stared intently at his eager audience for almost a minute before delivering his address entitled, "How to Write Successfully." It consisted of just one word. With great seriousness and emphasis he said, "Write!" Then he left the stage and the campus and returned to his home in another city.

At first the students were furious. No matter how accomplished or famous, he had no right to do this to them. They were expecting help. They wanted to become successful writers, and all he had to say was, "Write!" However, after some reflection they changed their opinion. The more they thought about it, the more they realized that he had an important point and that he had made it powerfully. Study, listening, and discussion can only take you so far in learning to write. If you want to learn to write, you have to actually do it. You have to sit down at your computer and put words and sentences and paragraphs together in a way that is inviting, interesting, and meaningful to readers. After you have done that repeatedly and conscientiously over time, you may

develop into a writer. Without that, you will not. Much the same must be said about witnessing. Reading, hearing, and discussion about it are helpful and usually necessary. However, *the way to become confident, comfortable, and effective in sharing Christ is to* ***do it*** *thoughtfully and faithfully, over and over again.*

Practice

1. Describe several acquaintances or relatives who seem very negative about Jesus.
2. What may have made each of them that way?
3. Consider strategies and ways to get through to each one.

TO DEB

Written by Milton L. Rudnick